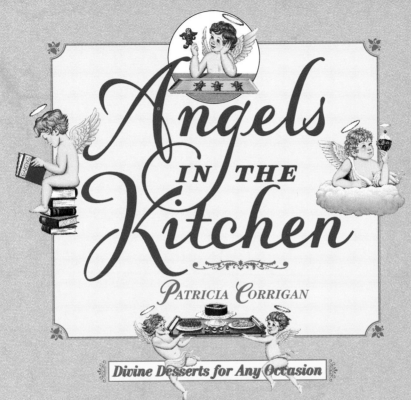

Angels
IN THE
Kitchen

PATRICIA CORRIGAN

Divine Desserts for Any Occasion

Illustrations by Joe Burleson

POCKET BOOKS

New York   London   Toronto   Sydney   Tokyo   Singapore

POCKET BOOKS, a division of Simon & Schuster Inc.
1230 Avenue of the Americas, New York, NY 10020

ISBN: 0-671-51711-2

First Pocket Books hardcover printing November 1994

10 9 8 7 6 5 4 3 2 1

POCKET and colophon are registered trademarks of
Simon & Schuster Inc.

Text design by Stanley S. Drate and
Ellen Gleeson/Folio Graphics Co., Inc.

Printed in the U.S.A.

*T*his book is dedicated to the memory of Ross Winter, my devilish Australian friend, who came into my kitchen bearing grated fresh ginger, a heavy hand with the hot sauce, and no taste for lettuce.

Acknowledgments

The late Bonnie Corrigan, Christine Andrews, Martha Baker, Allegra Cermak, Myra Grossman, Judy Guerrero, Linda P. Gwyn, Patrick Hart, Karen Manson, Perrin McEwen, Beth Remming, Ann Rothery, and the late Ruby Seay all shared truly celestial recipes. Madie Stroud, a home economist and a fine cook, kitchen-tested every recipe in this book. Thanks, too, to Jeanne Hanson, my agent, and Denise Silvestro, my editor, for their enthusiasm.

Contents

Candy

Introduction

This divine little book is brimming with heavenly dessert recipes guaranteed to transform you into "an angel in the kitchen," whether you make the recipes yourself or give the book to a friend as a gift.

Here are 26 delicious confections of a celebratory nature, including traditional angel food cake, tasty variations on that theme, creamy pies, angel cookies of the edible and ornamental kind, festive candies, rich coconut treats, and sumptuous chocolate desserts.

A home economist kitchen-tested every recipe, and every recipe comes complete with instructions that are easy to follow. Here, too, are baking tips to help ensure a successful outcome.

Angel lovers, dessert aficionados, cookbook collectors, and everyone who has ever declared, "That's heavenly!" after just one taste of something sweet will delight in this beautifully illustrated book.

Now let's get into the kitchen!

Cakes

Traditional Angel Food Cake

1¼ cups egg whites (from 8 or 9 large eggs), at room temperature
1 teaspoon cream of tartar
¼ teaspoon salt
1 teaspoon vanilla extract
1½ cups granulated sugar
1 cup sifted cake flour (sift before measuring)
Whipped cream frosting (or your favorite frosting)

In a large mixer bowl, beat egg whites on high speed until very stiff. Add cream of tartar, salt, and vanilla. Beat until egg whites form stiff peaks but are not dry. Add the sugar, 2 tablespoons at a time, beating well after each addition.

Sift the flour twice. Fold into egg whites.

Pour batter into an ungreased tube pan. Bake in a preheated 350° oven 45 minutes, or until cake tests done. Immediately invert pan and let cake cool completely—an hour or more. Loosen cooled cake from sides with knife or spatula, remove from pan, and frost if desired.

Whipped Cream Frosting

2 cups whipping cream
⅛ teaspoon salt
1 teaspoon vanilla extract
½ cup confectioners' sugar

Whip cream with salt and vanilla in an electric mixer or by hand until soft peaks form. Gradually add confectioners' sugar; continue beating until very stiff.
Spread frosting over cooled cake.

Serving suggestion: In strawberry season, you may want to cut the cake into 3 layers and top each layer with sweetened sliced strawberries. Cover berries with whipped cream frosting. Put layers back together and frost sides and top of cake with remaining frosting. Garnish with whole fresh strawberries.

Chocolate Angel Food Cake

¾   cup sifted cake flour
¼   cup unsweetened cocoa powder
1¼   cups egg whites (from 8 or 9 large eggs)
¼   teaspoon cream of tartar
1   teaspoon vanilla extract
1¼   cups granulated sugar
     Confectioners' sugar

Good things come in short packages—this cake boasts classic angel food texture and divine chocolate flavor, but it does not rise as high as store-bought cakes.

Sift flour and cocoa together 4 times. Set aside. Beat egg whites until foamy. Add cream of tartar and continue to beat until stiff enough to hold a peak. Fold in vanilla. Fold in sugar lightly, 2 tablespoons at a time. Sift small amounts of flour over mixture and fold in gently until all the flour is used.

Pour batter into an ungreased tube pan. Cut through batter with spatula to remove air bubbles. Bake in a 350° oven about 1 hour. Invert pan and let cake cool about 1 hour. Loosen cake from sides with a knife or spatula and remove from pan. Dust with light sprinkling of confectioners' sugar.

Pineapple Angel Delight

      1   large angel food cake
      1   envelope unflavored gelatin
      1   tablespoon cold water
      1   (15½-ounce) can crushed pineapple in its own juice
 4 to 6   tablespoons confectioners' sugar, to taste
      ½   teaspoon vanilla extract
     1½   cups whipping cream
           Fresh fruit, such as strawberries or kiwi, for garnish

A store-bought cake can be used, if you like. Split cake into 3 layers. Soften gelatin in cold water in top of double boiler. Drain pineapple, reserving juice. Add to gelatin with ⅓ cup drained juice, confectioners' sugar, and vanilla. Cook over hot water, stirring constantly, until gelatin dissolves. Chill until thickened.

Whip cream until stiff; gently fold into pineapple mixture. Spread mixture between layers and on top and sides of cake. Chill until ready to serve. Garnish with fresh fruit.

Chocolate-Filled Angel Food Cake

1   angel food cake
6   tablespoons unsweetened cocoa powder
6   tablespoons granulated sugar
⅛   teaspoon salt
3   cups heavy cream
1   cup toasted almond slivers, divided

Remove a 1-inch layer from top of cake. Scoop out center from cake, leaving walls and bottom about 1½ inches thick.

Mix the cocoa, sugar, and salt with the cream; chill for 1 hour. Whip cocoa and cream mixture until stiff. Fold in half the almonds. Fill cake with ⅓ of cocoa mixture. Place top on cake and frost with remaining cocoa mixture. Sprinkle remaining almonds on top of cake.

Chill 2 to 3 hours before serving.

Raspberry Angel Food Cake

  1   angel food cake
  1   (3½-ounce) can flaked coconut, divided
1½   cups frozen raspberries with juice, defrosted
  ½   teaspoon vanilla extract
  2   tablespoons granulated sugar
  2   cups whipping cream, whipped, divided

Remove a 1-inch layer from top of cake. Scoop out center from cake, leaving walls and bottom about 1 inch thick.

Crumble the scooped-out cake. Mix with ½ cup coconut, raspberries, vanilla, sugar, and 1 cup whipped cream. Fill cake with fruit mixture and replace top. Chill several hours.

Before serving, frost cake with remaining whipped cream. Sprinkle with remaining coconut.

Peppermint Ice Cream Angel Food Cake

1 angel food cake
½ gallon peppermint ice cream, softened
1 (12-ounce) can evaporated milk
2 cups granulated sugar
3 (1-ounce) squares unsweetened baking chocolate, chopped
1 teaspoon vanilla extract

Remove a 1-inch layer from top of cake. Scoop out center from cake, leaving walls and bottom about 1 inch thick.

Spoon ice cream into cake. Replace top. Put cake in freezer until ice cream is frozen again.

Make a hot fudge sauce: Mix together milk, sugar, chocolate, and vanilla in a heavy saucepan. Bring to a simmer over low heat and cook 5 minutes.

Drizzle hot or warm sauce over individual servings of cake.

Citrus Sponge Cake

  ³⁄₄   cup egg yolks (from 10 or 11 large eggs) at room temperature
  ½   cup water
  1   teaspoon lemon extract
  1   cup granulated sugar
1½   cups sifted cake flour (sift before measuring)
  ½   teaspoon baking powder
  ¼   teaspoon salt
1½   teaspoons grated lemon rind

This is an old-fashioned sponge cake—dense and rich in citrus flavor—and it does not bake up as high as store-bought cakes.

Line bottom of a tube pan with wax paper cut to fit.

Beat egg yolks with electric mixer 15 minutes, or until thick and lemon colored. Add water, lemon extract, and sugar; beat 15 minutes more. Sift flour, baking powder, and salt together 3 times. Fold flour mixture into yolk mixture; add lemon rind and mix.

Pour batter into ungreased pan. Bake in a preheated 350° oven 45 minutes, or until cake tests done. Immediately invert pan; let cake cool completely—about an hour. To remove from pan, loosen cake from sides of pan with a knife or spatula.

Frost cooled cake with a tart lemon-flavored frosting or your favorite frosting.

Pies

Lemon Angel Pie

4   eggs, separated
¼   teaspoon cream of tartar
1½   cups granulated sugar, divided
3   tablespoons lemon juice
2   teaspoons grated lemon zest
2   cups whipping cream
2   tablespoons confectioners' sugar

Beat egg whites until frothy. Add cream of tartar and beat until soft peaks form. Gradually add 1 cup of sugar, beating until egg whites are stiff and glossy. Spread over bottom and sides of a 9-inch pie pan. Bake in a 275° oven for 20 minutes. Increase oven to 300°; bake 40 minutes longer.

Combine egg yolks, ½ cup sugar, lemon juice, and lemon zest in the top of a double boiler. Cook until thick; remove from stove and allow to cool. Whip the cream with the confectioners' sugar. Blend half the whipped cream with the lemon mixture and spread into cooled meringue shell. Top with remaining whipped cream. Refrigerate 24 hours before serving.

Cherry Halo Pie

FOR CRUST:

- 2 cups all-purpose flour
- 1 teaspoon salt
- ⅔ cup chilled hydrogenated vegetable shortening
- 2 tablespoons chilled butter or margarine
- 5 tablespoons chilled orange juice
- Granulated sugar and ground cinnamon

FOR FILLING:

- 2 (16-ounce) cans tart cherries, drained
- 1 cup cherry liquid drained from cans
- 2 tablespoons quick-cooking tapioca
- ⅛ teaspoon salt
- 1 tablespoon all-purpose flour
- ¼ cup packed dark brown sugar
- ¾ cup granulated sugar

1   tablespooon Kirsch (cherry liqueur)
1   teaspoon almond extract
1   tablespoon butter, sliced

To make this crisp and tender crust, combine flour and salt and cut in shortening and butter with a pastry cutter. Add orange juice. Stir until mixture forms a ball.

This recipe makes a bottom crust and a halo for 2 pies. Divide the dough in half and reserve half for a second pie.

Roll out half the dough on a lightly floured surface. Using a 6-inch round bowl as a guide, cut out a circle of dough (the halo) and set aside. Roll out remaining dough and fit in the bottom of a 9-inch pie pan.

Dust the halo with sugar and cinnamon, 1 teaspoon of each or to taste. Place on a baking sheet and bake in a 450° oven until golden brown, about 7 to 10 minutes. Set aside to cool.

To make the filling, combine the cherry liquid with the tapioca. In another bowl, mix cherries, salt, flour, brown sugar, granulated sugar, Kirsch, and almond extract. Add the cherry liquid mixture.

Pour filling into pie shell. Dot with slices of butter. Bake in a 450° oven 10 minutes. Reduce oven to 350° and bake about 35 minutes more.

After pie cools, place cooled halo on top and serve.

Divine Pineapple Pie

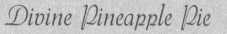

FOR SHELL:

2	egg whites
¼	teaspoon cream of tartar
	Dash of salt
½	teaspoon vanilla extract
½	cup granulated sugar

FOR FILLING:

1	cup granulated sugar
¼	cup cornstarch
	Dash of salt
1	(20-ounce) can crushed pineapple, packed in its own juice
2	tablespoons lemon juice
2	tablespoons butter
2	egg yolks, slightly beaten
1	cup whipping cream, whipped

To prepare shell: Combine egg whites, cream of tartar, salt, and vanilla; beat until foamy. Gradually add sugar, about 1 tablespoon at a time, beating constantly until mixture is very stiff and glossy. Spread on bottom and sides of buttered 9-inch pie pan. Bake in a preheated 275° oven 1 hour. Allow shell to cool thoroughly.

To prepare filling: In a saucepan, combine sugar, cornstarch, and salt. Gradually stir in undrained pineapple, lemon juice, and butter. Cook over medium heat, stirring constantly, until thickened. Add just a little of the hot pineapple mixture to egg yolks; combine with the rest of the hot pineapple mixture in saucepan. Cook 1 to 2 minutes more. Chill until cold.

Fold pineapple mixture into whipped cream. Pour filling into shell. Chill 3 hours before serving.

Cookies

Cream Cheese Angel Cut-Out Cookies

1	cup (2 sticks) margarine
1	(3-ounce) package cream cheese
1	cup granulated sugar
1	egg yolk
½	teaspoon vanilla extract
2½	cups all-purpose flour

Cream together the margarine and cream cheese. Add sugar and egg yolk; beat well. Stir in vanilla. Gradually sift in flour until thoroughly mixed. Chill.

Roll out half the dough on a lightly floured surface. Refrigerate remaining dough until you need it. With your favorite angel cookie cutter, cut out cookies. Transfer to ungreased cookie sheet. Bake in a 350° oven 10 to 12 minutes, until golden brown.

The size of the cookie cutter determines the yield, but no matter how many you get, you'll love the creamy texture of these pretty cookies.

Angelic Sugar Cookies

1   cup hydrogenated vegetable shortening
1   cup granulated sugar
2   eggs, beaten
2   teaspoons vanilla extract
1   cup sour cream
5   cups cake flour
2   teaspoons baking powder
1   teaspoon salt
1   teaspoon baking soda
    Crystal sugar (plain or colored)

Cream shortening and granulated sugar with an electric mixer until fluffy.

In another bowl, combine eggs, vanilla, and sour cream.

Sift together the flour, baking powder, salt, and baking soda. Add the flour mixture to the shortening and sugar mixture, alternating with the sour cream mixture. Allow dough to chill.

Divide dough into 3 equal parts and work with one part at a time. (Refrigerate the dough you're not working with so it doesn't get warm and sticky.) Roll out dough to about ⅛ inch thick on a pastry cloth lightly dusted with 4 tablespoons flour and 8 tablespoons granulated sugar.

Cut cookies with your favorite angel cookie cutter (available at cookware stores and many gift shops) or cut around a cardboard pattern you've made yourself. Sprinkle cookies lightly with crystal sugar. With a clean spatula, transfer cut-out cookies to an ungreased cookie sheet.

Bake in a 350° oven about 15 minutes or until cookies are golden brown. Remove cookies from pan immediately—otherwise, they will stick forever.

Yield: About 100 cookies, but it all depends on the size of the cutter.

Scandinavian Gingerbread Angels

2¼   cups granulated sugar
⅜   cup dark corn syrup
1¼   tablespoons ground cinnamon
2   teaspoons ground cloves
1   tablespoon ground ginger
1   cup (2 sticks) plus 2 tablespoons margarine
½   teaspoon baking soda
8   cups all-purpose flour

In a saucepan, combine sugar, corn syrup, cinnamon, cloves, and ginger with ¾ cup water. Place over moderate heat and stir until sugar is dissolved. Remove from heat. Add margarine and stir until mixture cools. Dissolve baking soda in tablespoon of water and add to mixture. Add flour gradually, working until dough is firm.

Lightly oil angel cookie mold (see note) or season with cooking oil spray. Wipe off excess with paper towel. Press a fistful of dough onto the center of mold; flatten out toward the edges. Roll across mold with a rolling pin. Remove excess dough with a sharp knife. Turn mold upside down over greased cookie sheet and let cookie fall out. Repeat with remaining dough.

Bake in a 350° oven 12 to 15 minutes. If cookies get too brown, they get hard—just dip them in coffee or milk.

You'll get 12 to 13 large cookies.

Note: For information on where to buy angel cookie molds, call a cookware store near you. Hartstone Inc. makes five different angel molds that can be used to make cookies or ornaments. For a catalogue, send $3 to Hartstone, P.O. Box 2626, Zanesville, OH 43702.

Celestial Chocolate-Covered Cherry Cookies

1½	cups all-purpose flour
½	cup unsweetened cocoa powder
¼	teaspoon salt
¼	teaspoon baking powder
¼	teaspoon baking soda
½	cup (1 stick) butter or margarine, softened
1	cup granulated sugar
1	egg
1½	teaspoons vanilla extract
1	(10-ounce) jar maraschino cherries (about 48)
1	(6-ounce) package semisweet chocolate morsels
½	cup sweetened condensed mix
4 to 5	teaspoons reserved cherry juice

In a large bowl, stir together flour, cocoa, salt, baking powder, and baking soda. In mixer bowl, beat together butter and sugar on low speed until fluffy. Add egg and vanilla; beat well. Gradually add dry ingredients to creamed mixture and beat until well blended.

Shape dough into 1-inch balls. Place balls on ungreased cookie sheet. Press down center of each ball with thumb. Drain cherries, reserving juice. Place a cherry in indentation in center of each cookie.

You frost these cookies *before* you bake them. To prepare frosting, combine chocolate morsels and sweetened condensed milk in a saucepan. Heat until chocolate melts. Stir in 4 teaspoons of the reserved cherry juice. Frosting will be thick. Spoon about 1 teaspoon of frosting over each cherry, spreading to cover cherry. (Frosting may be thinned slightly with more cherry juice.)

Bake in a preheated 350° oven about 10 minutes or until cookies are done. Set cookie sheet on top of a wire rack and allow cookies to cool about 5 minutes. Then carefully remove cookies from cookie sheet to continue cooling. Makes about 48 cookies.

Festive Apricot Nut Balls

1½ cups dried apricots, chopped
½ cup coarsely chopped pecans
2 cups shredded coconut
⅔ cup sweetened condensed milk
  Confectioners' sugar

In a mixing bowl, combine apricots, nuts, and coconut. Blend in condensed milk. Refrigerate for 1 hour. Shape mixture into 1-inch balls and roll in confectioners' sugar. Refrigerate another hour or so before serving.

Makes about 3 dozen cookies.

Angel Cookie Ornaments

2   cups all-purpose flour
½   cup salt
12 tablespoons hot tap water
¼   cup powdered instant tea mix

These cookies are not edible but they make wonderful Christmas tree ornaments.

Combine flour, salt, water, and tea mix in a bowl. Knead until dough is smooth and firm. Adjust the amount of flour or water until the feel is just right. (If the dough seems dry, wet your hands and knead some more.)

Follow directions on your favorite cookie mold to form the ornaments. While working with a cookie, cover bowl of dough with a damp cloth. After unmolding, poke a hole in the top of the ornament with 1 tine of a 2-tine fork or place a paper clip at the top for easy hanging. With a wet finger, smooth off any rough edges.

Bake in a 275° oven 1 hour or until ornaments are hard. Allow to cool. Decorate ornaments or varnish them plain. Allow to dry completely before hanging.

Makes about 4 ornaments.

Old-Fashioned Pound Cake

2¼ cups all-purpose flour
½ teaspoon salt
½ teaspoon baking soda
2 cups granulated sugar
1 teaspoon vanilla extract
1 teaspoon grated lemon zest
1 cup (2 sticks) butter or margarine, softened
3 eggs
1 (8-ounce) carton sour cream

In a large bowl, combine flour, salt, and baking soda. In another bowl, mix together sugar, vanilla, and lemon zest. Combine with flour mixture. Add butter, eggs, and sour cream. Mix at low speed on an electric mixer. Then beat for 3 minutes on medium speed.

Pour into a greased and floured 12-cup Bundt pan. Bake in a 325° oven for 60 to 70 minutes or until cake springs back when lightly touched.

Celestial Orange Chocolate Cheesecake

FOR CRUST:

    1½   *cups very finely chopped pecans*
    ⅓   *cup granulated sugar*
    2   *tablespoons melted butter*
        Dash of orange-flavored liqueur

FOR CAKE:

    3   *(8-ounce) packages cream cheese, softened*
    1   *cup granulated sugar*
    3   *eggs*
    6   *ounces unsweetened chocolate, melted*
    7   *ounces semisweet chocolate, melted*
    ⅓   *cup orange-flavored liqueur*
    1   *cup whipping cream*

To make crust: Combine pecans, sugar, and butter; press into the bottom and partly up the sides of a 9-inch springform pan.

Bake 10 minutes in a 350° oven. Sprinkle a bit of liqueur over warm crust and set aside to cool.

To make cake: Beat cream cheese with a mixer until fluffy. Gradually beat in sugar. Add eggs; beat once again. Add melted chocolate; mix well. Add liqueur. Fold in cream until blended.

Pour mixture into crust. Bake in a 325° oven 45 minutes to 1 hour. (You may want to put a drip pan or piece of foil in the bottom of the oven, as sometimes the cheesecake drips while baking.) Turn oven off and allow cheesecake to sit in oven for about 30 minutes longer.

Cool thoroughly before slicing.

Layered Chocolate Raspberry Brownies

FOR BROWNIES:

2	(10-ounce) bags chocolate raspberry morsels, *divided*
½	cup (1 stick) butter, *divided*
6	eggs, *divided*
2	cups all-purpose flour, *divided*
1	teaspoon baking powder, *divided*
½	teaspoon salt, *divided*

FOR RASPBERRY FILLING:

1	(12-ounce) bag frozen raspberries, *thawed*
1	cup granulated sugar

You will need to make 2 separate batches of the brownies.

To make first batch, melt half the morsels and half the butter in a large saucepan over low heat. Remove from stove and beat in 3 eggs with a spoon. Add half the flour, half the baking powder, and half the salt, stirring just until mixed. Spread batter in a greased 9-by-13-inch pan. Cover and place in freezer.

To prepare filling, combine raspberries and sugar in a blender or food processor; blend well. Set aside.

Prepare batter for the second batch of brownies using remaining ingredients. Remove first batch from freezer. Spread a layer of raspberry filling over frozen brownies. Spoon second batch of brownie mix over the raspberry filling, covering as much as possible.

Bake in a 350° oven for 25 to 30 minutes or until batter pulls away slightly from sides of pan. Cool completely in pan before cutting.

Frothy Strawberry Mousse

1   *pint strawberries*
3   *bananas, peeled and sliced*
2   *tablespoons honey*
3   *tablespoons fruit juice*
2   *tablespoons sour cream*
6   *walnut halves*

Wash berries. Set aside 6 for garnish. Hull remaining berries. In a blender, combine hulled strawberries, bananas, honey, and juice; mix well. Add sour cream; blend thoroughly.

Spoon this light, beautiful dessert into 6 wine glasses. Chill. Serve garnished with whole berries and walnuts.

Divine Coconut Delight

FOR CAKE:

1	box 2-layer mix for white cake
¼	cup vegetable oil
3	eggs
1	(8-ounce) carton sour cream
1	cup canned coconut cream

FOR FROSTING:

1	(1-pound) box confectioners' sugar
1	(8-ounce) package cream cheese, softened
2	tablespoons milk
1	teaspoon vanilla extract
1	(3½-ounce) can flaked coconut

In a large bowl, combine the cake mix, oil, eggs, sour cream, and coconut cream. Beat on medium speed until batter is smooth. Pour batter into a greased, floured 9-by-13-inch baking pan. Bake in a 350° oven 30 to 40 minutes, or until cake springs back.

To make the frosting, combine sugar, cream cheese, milk, and vanilla; mix well. Frost cooled cake. Sprinkle with coconut.

Tropical Angel Crush

1   (12-ounce) can cranberry juice concentrate
1   juice can of water
½   cup granulated sugar
1   (20-ounce) can crushed pineapple in its own juice, undrained
3   bananas, peeled and sliced thin
1   (10-ounce) package frozen strawberries or raspberries, packed
     in syrup

In a large bowl, combine cranberry juice concentrate, water, sugar, pineapple, bananas, and strawberries or raspberries. Mix well. Pour into a 9-by-13-inch baking pan and place in freezer overnight. Scoop individual servings into pretty dishes and serve.

Candy

Heavenly Hash

100 miniature marshmallows
  1 pound milk chocolate
  1 cup chopped pecans

In the top of a double boiler or in the microwave oven, melt chocolate. Allow chocolate to cool just a bit—otherwise, the hot chocolate will melt the marshmallows.

Line an 8-inch-square pan with waxed paper. Pour half the chocolate into the pan. Sprinkle marshmallows and nuts over the chocolate. Pour remaining chocolate over all. Allow to cool completely.

Break candy into pieces to serve.

Chocolate Mint Fudge

⅔   cup evaporated milk
1⅔ cups granulated sugar
½   teaspoon salt
1   teaspoon vanilla extract
1½ cups semisweet chocolate morsels
1½ cups chocolate mint morsels
1½ cups coarsely chopped pecans, divided

In a deep saucepan, combine the milk, sugar, and salt; bring to a boil. Remove from heat and stir in vanilla, chocolate morsels, chocolate mint morsels, and 1 cup nuts. Quickly spoon mixture into a lightly greased 8-by-8-inch baking pan. Sprinkle remaining ½ cup nuts over top and gently press into fudge.

Cool several hours and cut into squares to serve.

Divine Bourbon Balls

2 tablespoons unsweetened cocoa powder
1½ cups confectioners' sugar, divided
¼ cup bourbon whiskey
2 tablespoons light corn syrup
2½ cups crushed vanilla wafers (one 11-ounce box)
1 cup chopped pecans

Sift together the cocoa and 1 cup of the confectioners' sugar. Stir in bourbon and corn syrup. Add vanilla wafers and pecans; mix thoroughly (preferably with your hands).

Roll mixture into small balls. Roll balls in remaining confectioners' sugar. These can be eaten immediately or stored for several weeks in an airtight tin.

Makes 20–25 bourbon balls, depending on how big you make them.

Baking Tips

Baking Tips

➤ Read the entire recipe before you begin to bake, to make sure you have all the ingredients. You don't want to get almost through a recipe and then discover you're out of cream of tartar or chopped pecans.

➤ Use only the cleanest of baking pans. Angel food cakes, in particular, get testy and sometimes refuse to rise in pans with errant crumbs from cakes past. Cookies brown up nicest on clean, shiny pans, but you don't have to wash the pans between batches.

➤ Eggs beat up to their best volume if they are at room temperature. Separate eggs carefully—if any yolk gets into the white, the cake may not rise properly. (Cookware stores sell egg separators, but you can do this successfully without one. Gently crack the egg close to the center. Hold egg upright and remove top of shell. Tip the bottom part just enough so the white spills into a bowl. Carefully transfer the yolk between the top and bottom halves of the broken shell until all the white is out of the shell.)

➤ To cut an angel food cake without tearing it, use a serrated knife.

➤ Cake flour produces a lighter, more tender cake, but if you choose to substitute all-purpose flour, reduce the amount by 2 tablespoons.

➤ Always start the oven heating before you begin to make the recipe.

➤ Ovens vary, so keep in mind that baking time may vary. Set a timer and keep watch on whatever's in the oven (preferably through a window on the oven door—don't open the oven while you're baking). To test whether a cake is done, stick a toothpick in it. If it comes out clean, get that cake out of the oven.

➤ Pie dough and cookie dough roll best when chilled, and cut-out cookies transfer best on a wide metal spatula.

➤ Have fun!